BATS

BATS

by **George Shea**

illustrated by **Scott W. Earle**

EMC Corporation, St. Paul, Minnesota

PHOTO CREDITS

National Park Service: 15 (bottom)
Tom Stack & Associates—Leonard Lee Rue III: 15 (top)

Library of Congress Cataloging in Publication Data

Shea, George.
  Bats.

  (Four (not so) awful creatures)
  SUMMARY: Explains the facts and fiction about bats
proving that these nocturnal creatures do not deserve
their scary image.
    1. Bats—Juvenile literature. [1. Bats]
I. Earle, Scott W.   II. Title.   III. Series
QL737.C5S49   599'.4   77-23287
ISBN 0-88436-304-X
ISBN 0-88436-305-8 pbk.

Published by EMC Corporation
180 East Sixth Street
St. Paul, Minnesota 55101
Printed in the United States of America
0 9 8 7 6 5 4 3 2

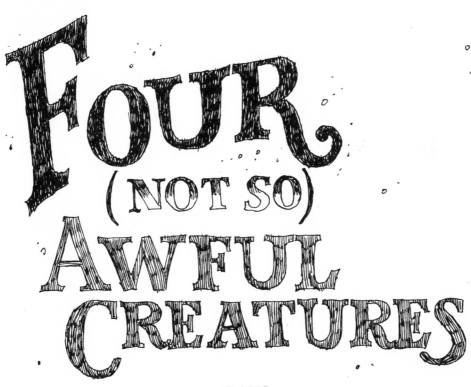

FOUR (NOT SO) AWFUL CREATURES

BATS
SPIDERS
WOLVES
ALLIGATORS

This book is all about BATS!
Most people don't like them.
Most people are scared stiff of them.
Most people think they're just BAD.
A lot of people think they should be WANTED, dead or alive.

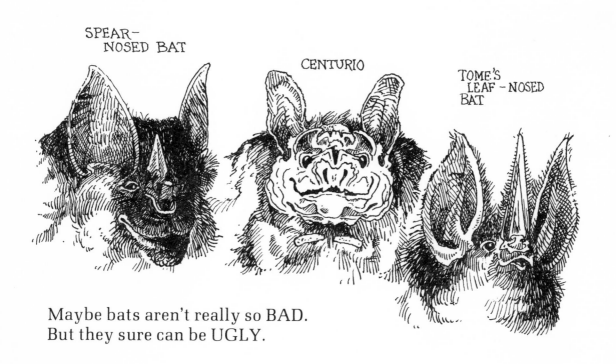

SPEAR-NOSED BAT

CENTURIO

TOME'S LEAF-NOSED BAT

Maybe bats aren't really so BAD.
But they sure can be UGLY.

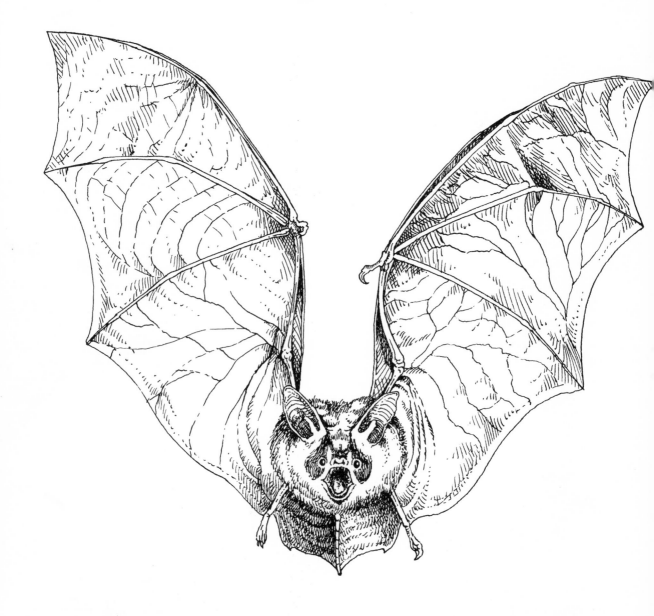

It's scary to see a bat coming right at you. Most people would run. Almost anyone would run. You can see why most people are afraid of bats.

1. Some of them are not very pretty.
2. The idea of a bat flying down at you is very frightening.

Question No. 1: Should people be afraid of bats?

Answer: No. There are only two reasons to be afraid of bats.

1. They may bite you.
2. If they bite you, they may make you sick.

But these two fears don't make much sense.

First, bats don't go around biting people. Bats are more afraid of people than people are afraid of bats.

Yes, every now and then, a bat bites someone. But it doesn't happen often. When it happens, it is often because someone has bothered a bat—chased it, hunted it, or frightened it.

Second, even if a bat bites you, it will probably not make you sick.

Some animals have a disease called *rabies*. When they bite another animal, they pass the disease on to the animal. Rabies is a very bad disease. It is very painful. It often ends in death.

People are afraid that bats have rabies. Some do . . . but very few . . . very, very few. Maybe one bat in a thousand . . . Maybe one in ten thousand. *Cows* are more likely to have rabies than bats. So are cats and dogs. Don't worry about it. Very, very few cows or dogs or cats have rabies. And even fewer bats do.

Question No. 2: But what if a bat flies (swoops) down at you?

Answer: No big deal. Many bats will do this just to see what you are. They don't do it so they can bite you. They may fly very close by you. But they will almost never bite you.

Question No. 3: But aren't bats ugly?

Answer: Yes, some of them are. And what's so bad about being ugly? Besides, the ugliest bats aren't even found in North America.

So, unless you travel to Central or South America, home of the wrinkle-faced bat, the spear-nosed bat, and Tome's leaf-nosed bat, you won't meet them. And probably most people who *do* live there don't ever see them.

There are worse things in this world than being ugly. And, anyway, if *you* were a bat, perhaps you would think that *people* were pretty ugly. You never know. You might. For one thing, people don't look very pretty when they're scared stiff.

That's the way people look when they see a bat. And that's the way a bat sees them.

RED BAT

FLYING FOX BAT

Besides, a lot of bats are pretty cute.

Question No. 4: But don't bats drink blood? *People's* blood?

Answer: Yes, some bats do drink blood. But very few do. And they almost never drink people's blood. They go after the blood of animals, such as cows and horses and other farm animals. There are about 850 different kinds of bats in the world. But only one kind, the *vampire* bat, drinks blood.

And it doesn't live in the United States or Canada either. Vampire bats live in Mexico and in Central and South America. They live as far north as Central Mexico and as far south as Argentina.

VAMPIRE BAT

They're quite a problem down there. When a vampire bat takes blood from an animal, it takes very little. It takes only about an ounce— about as much as you could fit on a large spoon.

But there are *thousands*, even *millions* of vampire bats going out every night. And if every one of them drinks an ounce of blood . . . that's a lot of blood. The bats take blood again and again from the same animals. In time, they can make the animals weak.

This is how a vampire bat does its thing.

By day, it sleeps in a cave with thousands of other bats. It hangs upside down on the wall of the cave. When night comes, the bat—and all the other bats—leaves the cave. It flies off in search of blood.

It sees a herd of sleeping cows. It picks one out. It flies down and lands. And then it does a strange thing. Little by little, it sneaks up on the cow on *foot*.

When it's right next to the cow, it very quietly flies up in the air again. And it comes down, very softly and lightly, on the sleeping cow's body. So far, the cow is still asleep and doesn't know what is about to happen.

Then the vampire bat strikes. It makes a small cut with its two sharpest front teeth. It doesn't *suck* the animal's blood. It *licks* it from the cut it has made. And, most of the time, the cow doesn't even wake up.

Vampire bats do a lot of damage. Very few bats carry rabies. But vampire bats often do. When they bite the cows, they give the disease to the cows. Many of the cows get very sick. Some die.

Scientists have found a new and strange way to kill vampire bats. They go out and catch a few of them. Then they put a drug on the bats' bodies. Then they let them go.

The bats fly back to their caves. Bats in caves lick one another, the way cats do. Every bat who licks the body of a bat carrying the drug dies. The drug makes them bleed inside. This is how they die.

VAMPIRES

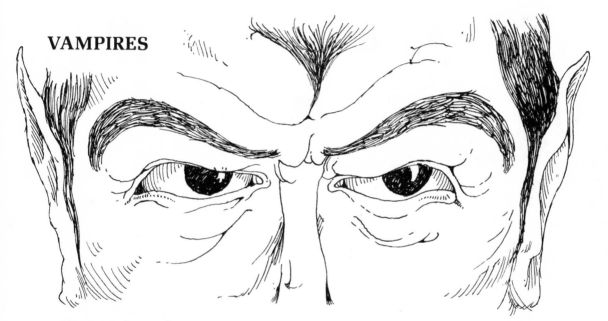

Now, what about VAMPIRES?

Are there really such things as vampires? Of course not. But, like a lot of other strange things, they're fun to believe in.

The idea of vampires got started long ago in Central Europe among a people called the *Slavs*. The Slavs lived in places that are now parts of Russia, Poland, Yugoslavia, Rumania, and some other countries in Central Europe. One of those places is a part of Rumania called Transylvania.

The Slavs believed that some dead people rose out of their graves. These people, these "living" dead, were called *vampires*. This was a very strong belief among the Slavs. Though, of course, it wasn't true.

One of the leaders of the Slavs was a man called Vlad Dracula. For a time, between 1456 and 1462, Dracula ruled in Transylvania. He was a very cruel ruler. He killed thousands of people. And so, when people thought of him, they thought of blood. But, for hundreds of years, no one outside of Transylvania or the Slavic countries thought much about Dracula or vampires.

Then, in 1897, an English writer named Bram Stoker wrote a book. He called it *Dracula.* It was all about Count Dracula, a man who was a vampire. He went around drinking other people's blood, and turning them into vampires. And . . . he could change himself into a bat. The story wasn't true, of course.

But people liked to read it. They bought a lot of copies of Mr. Stoker's book. In 1931 a movie called *Dracula* came out. It told pretty much the same story that was told in the book. A lot of people went to see the movie. And, since then, a lot of other vampire movies have been made.

But do these movies really have anything to do with bats? No. Not really.

Vampire bats are very real. But human vampires are only in movies. Besides, the vampire bat is only one kind of bat. One out of 850. The vampire is only one kind of person. A make-believe person.

Now, what about all the other 849 or so kinds of bats?

The kind of bat we see the most in the United States and Canada is the little brown bat.

The little brown bat is found in all parts of the world. It's small, only about two inches long. Little brown bats are not very big. But they make up for it in numbers. There are millions of them in North America.

Many of them live near people. They live in dark, out-of-the-way places. Some sleep in hollow trees, some in spaces between rocks, some in barns, and some in tops of churches.

But most bats live in caves. More than a million Mexican free-tailed bats live in the Carlsbad Caverns of New Mexico. It's quite a sight to see them leave the Caverns at sundown.

Bats usually live together in caves. But some bats, such as red bats, are loners. They stay to themselves. Red bats live alone in trees.

While it's true that most kinds of bats are afraid of people, this isn't true with little brown bats. Brown bats are the bats that may fly down close to your head. They do this not to bite you, but just to find out where you are.

But don't they know where you are already? Not quite. We'll explain.

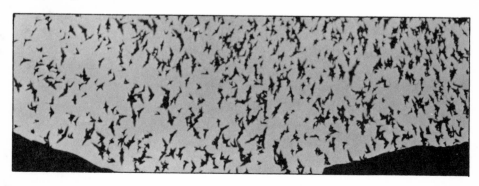

ARE BATS REALLY BLIND?

Bats can't see well from a distance. But they're far from blind. Perhaps you have heard someone use the saying, "blind as a bat." People are afraid of low-flying bats because they think bats can't see well. They fear the bats will bump into them. Some fear that a bat will fly into their hair and get caught there. But these fears don't make sense.

Bats are not at all blind. Some don't see well, even up close. But bats are much better at finding their way around in the dark than we are. They don't find their way around with their *eyes*, though.

How *do* bats find their way in the dark?

Two hundred years ago, an Italian scientist named Spallanzani tried to find out. He found that even *blind* bats could find their way in the dark.

Then he decided to make the bats *deaf*. He did this by stopping up their ears with plugs. After this, the bats couldn't do anything right. They were crashing into walls and chairs.

Then he took the plugs out. The bats could hear again. And they could find their way in the dark. And so, Spallanzani found that bats used their ears to find their way.

But how?

Years later, in the 1930s, an American student named Donald Griffin found the answer. Griffin found out that bats get around by listening to the sounds of their own voices. When bats fly they make sounds. Many of the sounds are so high-pitched that our ears can't hear them. These sounds strike something, such as a tree. The sounds bounce back. The bat hears the sounds that bounce back. By listening to these echoes, it finds its way.

You could do the same thing. (But you couldn't do it nearly as well as a bat). Pretend you're in a very dark room. You can't see anything. You want to find out where the wall is. You shout. The sound of your shout bounces off the nearest wall. This is the way you could find out where the wall is—by listening. And this is the way bats see in the dark—by listening.

Scientists are still trying to learn more about how bats hear. Their hearing is so wonderful that it's hard to believe. For one thing, we know that bats make 250 little sounds or "clicks" a second. Often, people can't hear these sounds. But bats can. And they use them.

A bat flies toward something, such as an insect. It makes hundreds of little "clicks" as it gets closer. The "clicks" bounce back. And the bat's little brain uses them to figure out where the insect is.

A bat's hearing is like our *sonar* or *radar*.

Sonar is a way of finding out where something is under water. Sound waves are sent down into the water. And, by the way they bounce back, we can tell where something is in the water.

Radar is a way of finding out where things are in the air. Electric waves are sent out into the air. By the way they bounce off of things, we can tell where something is in the air.

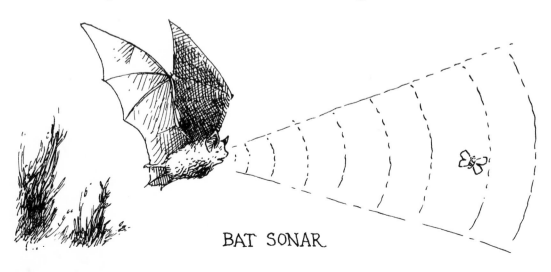

BAT SONAR

A bat's hearing is really more like *sonar* than radar. Radar uses electric waves. Sonar uses *sounds* (the same way that bats do).

When a bat swoops down at your head, it is using its hearing to find out where you are. First, it can tell that you are somewhere near. Then it comes down closer, sending out little "clicks" as it comes. They bounce off of you. They tell the bat where you are.

The bat has to come pretty close to find out where you are. But there's no need to worry. Bats almost never hit people. Or bite them. This is just the way they have of seeing in the dark—by listening.

Let's take a look at some of the different kinds of bats in the world.

BATS AROUND THE WORLD

Cannibal Bats

A *cannibal* is a person who eats other people. And so, a cannibal bat is a bat that eats other bats. It also eats insects (most bats eat insects), spiders, birds, frogs, lizards, and mice. The type of cannibal bat shown here lives mostly in Southeast Asia.

CANNIBAL BAT

This is another type of cannibal bat. It lives in Australia. It's a large bat. It's so light in color that they call it the *ghost bat.* Spooky.

GHOST BAT

There are cannibal bats in South America too. They attack small animals and other bats. But they seem to like people. They're tame and gentle with people. They make good pets. (But they should be kept away from other pets.)

Fisherman Bats

This is the *Noctilio.* It's found from Argentina north to Mexico and Cuba. It flies low over the water at night. It catches fish with its claws. If the fish are small, it eats them while it flies.

FISHERMAN
BAT

CENTURIO

Flower Bats

Here's one of those really ugly bats again. The *Centurio*, or wrinkle-faced bat, lives mostly in Central and South America.

When it sleeps, it covers its face with a fold of skin from under its chin.

Most of these bats eat fruit. Many also eat insects. Some eat flowers. And, like bees and butterflies, they drink *nectar* from flowers. *Nectar* is a sweet liquid that's found in flowers. Bees use it to make honey.

Long-nosed bats drink nectar from flowers too. These bats are found in Texas and Arizona in the summer. Here's a long-nosed bat about to drink nectar from a Saguaro flower.

LONG-NOSED BAT

These flowers are long and deep. Sometimes it's hard to get at the nectar down deep inside the flower. Sometimes, to get inside, a bat has to hold on to the flower with its arms and feet.

But the bat is gentle. It doesn't harm the flower. In one way, the bats really help the flowers. They help them to grow. When a bat comes away from a flower, its head is covered with *pollen*. Pollen helps flowers to grow. The bat brings the pollen to another flower . . . and another . . . and another. Bees and butterflies do the same thing.

Let's look at some other kinds of bats.

TRACHOPS

ROUSETTUS

FLYING FOX

The *Trachops* looks like a monster from another world.

The *Rousettus*, or dog-faced bat, looks more like a mouse to some people. The German word for bat is *Fledermaus*. It means "flying mouse."

The flying fox is the world's largest bat. Its wingspread is five to six feet. You don't have to worry about being attacked by a flying fox. It doesn't care for the taste of people. It eats fruit and the nectar from flowers. Anyway, it lives far away— around Australia and Southeast Asia. It looks very much like a fox. People in Southeast Asia, by the way, like the taste of it. They eat flying fox bats. There's a lot to eat. A flying fox body weighs from two to three pounds.

Flying foxes are good swimmers. Many live on islands in the South Pacific. To get from one island to the next, they sometimes swim.

HERE ARE SOME OTHER STRANGE LOOKING BATS!

1. This fruit-eating bat has a face like a horse.

2. This Latin-American bat has a snout like a pig.

3. A sheep? No, a sheath-tailed tomb bat from Australia.

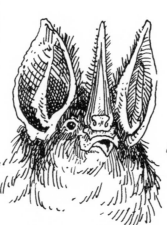

4. This bat looks like a rabbit. And, like a rabbit, it lives in forests.

5. Another monster from outer space: Tome's leaf-nosed bat.

6. This *Cheiromeles* looks like (take your pick):
   a. a skunk
   b. a hippo
   c. the front end of a bus

A BAT'S BODY

A helpful hint . . . Not that you probably will anyway . . . But, if you pick up a bat—don't pick it up by its wings. This won't really harm the animal, but it will cause it pain. Why? Because a bat's hands are in its wings.

Suppose you were caught by something much larger than you are . . . and it picked you up by your fingers. It would hurt. If you pick up a bat, pick it up by the back of its neck, or cradle its entire body.

Something else about bats . . . Something that makes them just like . . .

is that they are *mammals.*

> **mam-mal** (mam'əl) *n.* L. *mamma,* breast. One of a group of animals that has a backbone and nurses its babies with milk.

Mammals are the only animals with fur or hair. Bats have fur. But bats are the *only* mammals that fly. Who ever heard of a flying bear? All of which makes bats very different and unusual animals. They are the only animals that have both fur and wings.

A BAT SKELETON

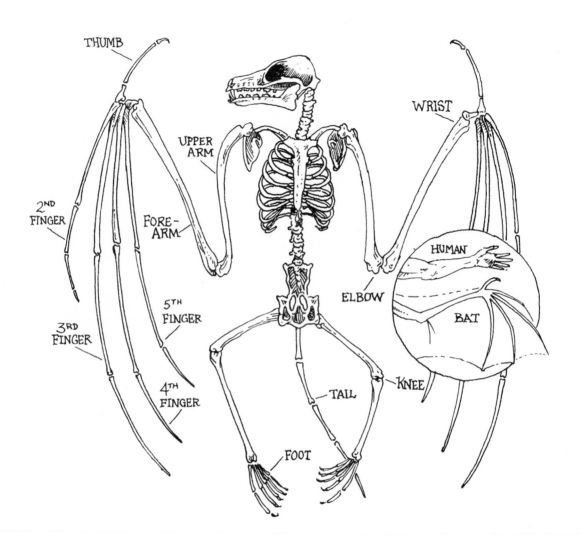

THUMB

WRIST

UPPER ARM

2ND FINGER

FORE-ARM

HUMAN

5TH FINGER

ELBOW

3RD FINGER

BAT

4TH FINGER

KNEE

TAIL

FOOT

A BAT GROWS UP

When a bat is born, its mother cradles it in the pocket of skin around her tail, the *tail membrane*. The bat mother, like other mammal mothers, has breasts that give milk. Bat babies have a special set of teeth. They are called "milk teeth." With its milk teeth, the bat baby is able to hang on to its mother when it's feeding at its mother's breast and when its flying through the air with its mother. The young bat hitches rides this way.

The little bat rides along with its mother only so long. In time it grows too heavy. Then the mother sets it down and flies off by herself.

The mother brings back food, probably crushed insects. Then there are flying lessons. And, in time, like everything else in the world, the little bat grows up. And goes off on its own.

A MOTHER RED BAT
CRADLING HER BABY
IN HER TAIL MEMBRANE

WHAT BATS EAT

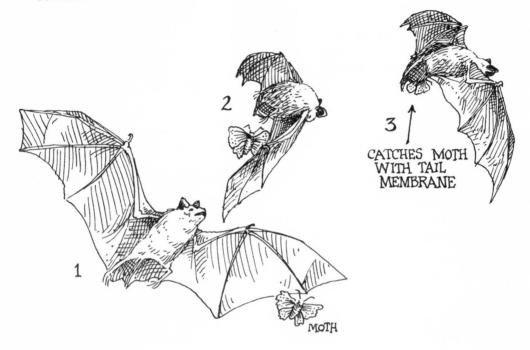

2

3

CATCHES MOTH
WITH TAIL
MEMBRANE

1

MOTH

Bats eat insects. A lot of insects. In one night, one bat may eat as many as 5,000 little insects. This is one of the ways bats help people. If it weren't for bats, there would be too many insects. Bats (and birds) eat many insects that do harm. They eat insects that harm plants and spread disease.

Bats have a neat way of catching insects. They *don't* catch them in their mouths. They trap them in their *tail membranes.* They catch them the way a ball player uses a glove to catch a ball.

The tail membrane folds around the insect. The bat may reach down with its head and eat the bug while it's flying. Or, if it's a big insect, it may take it home and eat it later.

Most North American bats eat insects. Flower bats eat nectar and flowers. Fisherman bats eat fish. Cannibal bats eat other bats as well as frogs, lizards, birds, and mice. Some bats are fruit eaters. Vampire bats eat only blood.

WHEN WINTER COMES

CLUSTERS OF BROWN BATS IN A CAVE

Bats are not cold-weather animals. They don't get around much in winter. Like many animals, they *hibernate* when winter comes. They go into their caves and stay there. Their bodies slow down. And, in a way, they "go to sleep" for the winter.

Some, but not many, fly south for winter. They fly south right along with the birds.

Some bats have a neat way of going places. They "hitch" rides aboard ships. A bunch of bats will fly onto a ship, and stay along for the ride.

In America, bats prefer the warmer south to the colder north. You're more likely to see a bat in Florida than in Maine.

FLYING SOUTH

BATS ARE LUCKY

Bats have pretty good lives. They live longer than most animals, for one thing. Every day, when a bat goes to sleep, its whole body slows down. Because of this, its body doesn't wear out easily. Some bats live twenty years or even longer. But most North American bats live only about two and one-half years. A mouse, which is about the same size as a bat, lives only one year.

Bats have few enemies. Few other animals hunt and eat them. Few can catch them. The bat's enemies are skunks, weasels, house cats, and oppossums. And owls. Owls sometimes wait for bats outside their caves and tree holes. They try to catch them as they come out. But they don't have much luck at it.

WHY BATS DON'T HAVE SO MANY BABIES

Bats don't have many babies. A bat mother gives birth only once a year—and usually to only one baby. This is a bit unusual among animals. A mouse, for example, gives birth six times in the one year that it's alive. Each time it may have six babies. But very few of the babies will live.

Bat babies have a much better chance of living. And bats live quite a long time. That's why bat mothers don't have so many babies.

A LOT OF BATS

There are a lot of bats in the world. There are more of them than almost any other kind of mammal. Of the mammals, only rodents (rats, mice, and so on) exist in larger numbers.

Why Bats Have Fairly Easy Lives:
- They have few enemies.
- Their enemies have a hard time catching them.
- They don't have many babies to care for.
- They don't have to work long hours to find food.
- They spend a lot of their time in deep sleep.
- Their bodies don't wear out easily.

HOW BATS HELP OUT

Bats do quite a lot to help make the Earth a better place to live. They eat a great number of insects. If it weren't for bats, there would be too many insects. Many of the insects they eat are insects that harm plants and people.

Flower bats help flowers to grow. They do this by spreading pollen around.

Bats' body wastes are very useful. The waste that drops from their bodies is called *guano*. It may be the world's best *fertilizer*.

And what is *fertilizer*?

fer-til-i-zer (fur'təl-iz'ər n. Something that is spread on the ground, mixed with soil. It makes the soil richer, and helps it to grow food.

SO WHY DON'T PEOPLE LIKE BATS

The reasons why people don't like bats go back a long way. For a long time, when people thought of the bat, they thought of darkness . . . and death . . . and evil . . .

Why? Why have people thought of the bat this way? For different reasons. One big reason is DARKNESS. Bats live in the DARK. By day they sleep in dark places—often in caves. By night they fly. And they get around so well in the darkness, they seem to rule the night.

Long ago, people thought of the night as a time of danger, of evil. They even thought that the night air was bad. They thought that breathing it could make you sick.

Even today, people still sometimes think of the night, of the dark, as bad. They are still afraid of it. Think of how afraid some children are of the dark. We are not at home in the dark. But a bat is.

Another reason the bat is thought of as bad is because it is so DIFFERENT . . . so UNUSUAL. It is a mammal and it has fur. But it flies. And it has wings. But it has no feathers, and is not a bird.

Long ago, people had special feelings about animals that were unusual. They thought that some of these animals were good. They thought that some were evil. They thought the bat was evil. Just because it was different. This was a simple belief. It was a stupid belief. (Just like the belief some people have that it's bad luck if a black cat walks in front of them.) But it was a very strong belief. And like a lot of strong, simple, stupid beliefs . . . it is still around. People still believe it.

In China, when people think of the bat, they think of good and happy things. A Wu-Fu is a pendant that some Chinese people wear around their necks. It is supposed to bring good luck. In China, bats are a sign of good luck.

The Japanese see them that way too. But we don't. Probably all those vampire movies don't help the way we think about bats.

A CHINESE WU-FU PENDANT... FOR GOOD LUCK

Then why do people go to those movies? Many people go because they enjoy being frightened. Think of all the movies that people go to see that frighten them.

Very few people are ever attacked by wild animals. No one is ever attacked by a monster. But people seem to enjoy being afraid.

Think about spiders. Many people scream when they see a spider. Any spider. But the great majority of spiders are not harmful.

It's the same with bats. It's an old idea—the idea that bats are frightening and very ugly. We even began this book that way—with pictures of some "ugly" bats. Pictures such as those can be hard to forget. But so are pictures such as these. . .

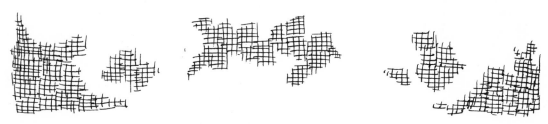

Bats can be beautiful!

THE PAINTED BAT HAS LONG, BRIGHT, REDDISH-YELLOW FUR...

THE BEAUTIFUL HOARY BAT IS CALLED THE SILVER-HAIRED BAT...

THE FLYING FOX HAS BEAUTIFUL ORANGE AND BROWN FUR...

THE RED BAT HAS BRIGHT YELLOW-ORANGE FUR, FROSTED WITH WHITE...

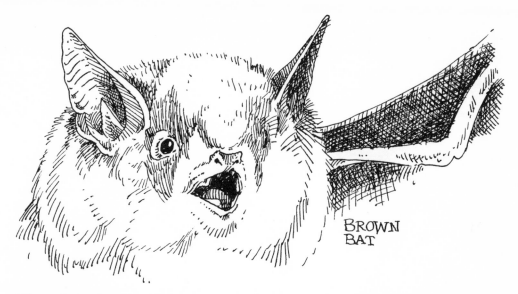

BROWN
BAT

The plain brown bats we see here in North America may not be beautiful, but they are cute and easy to like.

Dr. David Mork teaches about bats at St. Cloud State University in Minnesota. He spends a lot of time around bats. He likes bats so much that he would like other people to like them too. He knows that a lot of young people have wrong ideas about bats. He wants them to like and respect bats—and not be afraid of them.

BROWN
BAT

People usually don't like the things they're afraid of.
That's why Dr. Mork sometimes visits schools. And when he
does, he takes some bats with him. He lets the bats free in the
classroom. They fly around the room. They land on walls and
chairs. The students pick them up. They learn not to fear them.
They find out that bats like to be scratched, petted, and fed.
And like other animals . . . (and people) . . . they yawn,
they sneeze, they wink.

It may not be a good idea to go walking around in bat caves. But it's not a good idea to go around your whole life being afraid of bats. Bats and people are not enemies. Bats will probably never become as close to us as dogs and cats. We have our world. And they have theirs. But we are both a part of the same world.

There are so many things in this world to like and respect.
And bats are among those things . . .

INDEX